Many people say, "Don't judge a book by its cover." I would say, "Don't judge a book by its size!"

This is a concise, usable, "do it today" kind of book.

Rae Wilson has managed to incorporate techniques and exercises into this book, which allow the reader to take control of their lives with noticeable and quick results. It is filled with easy to understand, but also deep questions, that can take the reader into an awareness of what they have been creating in their lives.

So, don't be fooled by the "size", there is so much meat in here that you will be "dining" on it for years. Each time you come up against the person who you are versus the person you are striving to be, take out this book, do the exercises and you'll find yourself moving forward and becoming the better, more improved version of yourself.

— Linda Lynch-Johnson, International
Expert of Change, Author of *The Adapter Factor:
When Change Scares the Hell Out of You*

BE YOUR MOST INFLUENTIAL SELF
IN EVERY SITUATION

POWER. PERFORMANCE. PRESENCE. PERSUASION.

RAE WILSON

Published by P4 Training Solutions
www. P4TrainingSolutions.com

Printed in the United States of America.
Cover and layout design by Chelsea Jewell.

ISBN: 978-1720571285

To Christian and Cameron,
Thank you for being my sons,
teaching me many life lessons,
and giving me a reason
to want to be my best self.

And to Jessica, you are
like a daughter to me.

Special Thanks to
Louise,
You effortlessly embody
Love, compassion and fun!
You are my greatest supporter
and biggest cheerleader.

"Yesterday, I was clever, so I wanted to change the world. Today, I am wise, so I am changing myself."

— Rumi

Contents

Introduction

Like many people, for years I walked around with the feeling of a hole in my heart or in my gut and a sense that something is missing. Something isn't right, but I cannot put my finger on it. I need that "thing" to fill the hole — that small, persistent yearning that was always there.

Well, the one thing about me is that I'm the most persistent person I know. I knew something was missing. I knew something wasn't the way it should be and I decided that I was going to figure it out.

Of course, like most people, I look a lap (or two) around the outside world looking for what would fill this hole. I married the most handsome man that I had ever laid eyes on. (Hmm… that didn't do it). I climbed the corporate ladder and held what I thought was a really important job. (Not it!) I made lots of money. (Nope). I bought a big fancy house and had several luxury cars. I was right up there with the Jones. (No, the hole is still there). I divorced the most handsome man I'd ever seen. (Not it). I married another extremely handsome man. (Again, that didn't do it). Oh, and there were lots of ups and downs along the way. While each of those steps brought me a little satisfaction for a moment, it was very short lived until the hole made its presence known again.

After a bunch of side trips along the path, I started looking on the inside. I started to find answers and solutions that felt good and made a lasting difference. The hole was shrinking.

I'm the kind of person that has to dig deep and get to the bottom of things, if there is such a thing as a bottom. In this process, I studied lots of religions, philosophies, science, physics and metaphysics. You name it. I studied it. I'm pretty sure that I have every self-help or personal development book ever written. I also have every spiritual book and Bible ever written. (I'm exaggerating, but you get the idea). If there was a workshop or program, I was there. In the process, I found some true solutions that really made a permanent difference. I used the information to fundamentally change myself, or really, to find who I was all along.

Now, this little book is not intended to go deeply into science, physics, philosophy or religion. I will leave that to the authorities. This book is primary intended to give you simple concepts and solutions that you can implement right now — to make a difference in the moment. Lots of this information, I picked up along my path from other sources. Where possible, I cited the reference. A lot of the information came from all my reading, studying and workshops so who knows the original source. Much of this information came from my inner wisdom. I'm not claiming to be the only person to discover it. I'm just presenting what I have learned from my journey. I hope that this material is helpful to you.

If you look at the world and try to figure it out and apply outer action to achieve results, you are certainly doing it "the hard way". (I consider myself an expert in the "hard way". In fact, I have a PhD in the School of Hard Knocks, which I am grateful for. It propelled me to become who I am today). While action does work to a certain extent, what really works about the action is the underlying principles that you are unwittingly employing. If you learn the basic principles, the action happens much more easily.

BE WHO YOU WANT TO BE TODAY

Be more concerned with your character than your reputation, because your character is what you really are, while your reputation is merely what others think you are.

— *John Wooden*

I have wonderful news for you. You have absolute, complete and total control of who you are without exception! For the moment, that is great news for you. Of course, if you are not that fond of "who you are", the bad news is that you are completely responsible for that too. But, you can absolutely become the person you want to be and this book is designed to tell you how. And, it is truly very simple, although not necessarily easy.

Let me start by telling you who you are not. You are not the person that you think you are. You are not the person in the mirror. You are not your body. You are not the name you were given. You are also not your behavior. You are not your behavior - you *do* behavior.

Many people identify themselves with their behavior. For some reason, this is especially true if it is behavior that they don't like. This identity doesn't allow them to make room for new behavior. You are not your behavior. In fact, anything that can "change" is not who you are. How could it be? It cannot be who you are at the core if you can change it. It is just who you are "being" in this moment.

In truth, you are only the person you are being right now because your *thinking* matches the person you believe yourself to be. Here is the great news. If you change your thinking, you will be the new person that matches your new thinking. This is not a religious book in any way, but the Bible makes my point well when it says, "create in me a new man, Oh Lord." What this is really saying is create new thinking in me that will result in new behavior.

More simply, you are the driver of the car — not the car itself. If you drive a Jeep, you don't consider yourself a Jeep. If you drive a BMW, you don't consider yourself the BMW. If you drive a Toyota Corolla, you don't consider yourself that car either. You know that it is just the outer vehicle and you are the person that is operating it.

The part of you that is who you really are, is the person operating your outer vehicle, not the vehicle itself. So, this book is about the inside you, not the "body vehicle" you are driving around in. At this point, you might be thinking, isn't that just semantics? Really, what difference does that distinction make?

You are consciousness having a physical experience. What determines the experience that you have is your thinking. Your behavior is a result of your thinking. If your thinking changes, your behavior will change too. You are who you think you are in this moment.

Your life experience is equal to your thinking. If you decide that you would like to have a different life experience, you now must "put on" or adopt new thinking to match the person that you want to be. No, your physical appearance won't change, but your inner experience will be totally transformed. (Of course, if your underlying belief about being an overweight person changed, your physical appearance would conform to your new belief). When this happens, you will have a new experience of your outer being too. In other words, the old adage "as above, so below," "as within, so without" and vice versa is true. Your inner thinking will determine your outer experience.

Now that you know that by changing your thinking, you will change your life experience, let's explore who you want to be in this life. Who do you want to be? Who do you admire in life? Who do you admire in history? If you could be anyone, who would you be? You might say, "there are many people that I admire and would like to be like." Great! You can identify the best characteristics of all these people and use them as your basis for creating your new self.

These are important questions to ponder because once you have identified who you admire, who you would like to be like, now all you have to do is adopt their thinking in order to become your own version of that person or combination of people.

That may sound pretty simple, but it will take tremendous effort and great persistence to actually pull it off. Why? The average person thinks over 60,000 thoughts per day, so it will take considerable will, effort and dedication to adopt a new way of thinking. It can be done.

A great way to stay committed to "putting on" this new person is to identify "why" you want to become this new person. Why do you admire that person or these people? What is it about them that you aspire to be like? Whoever they have become in life or whatever they have achieved is a result of their inner thinking. Here is a list of admirable characteristics you may want to adopt or "put on":

Adventurous	Fair	Loyal
Amiable	Faithful	Magnanimous
Appreciative	Flexible	Optimistic
Benevolent	Focused	Passionate
Brilliant	Forgiving	Peaceful
Calm	Friendly	Persuasive
Caring	Fun	Playful
Charismatic	Generous	Reliable
Charming	Genuine	Resourceful
Cheerful	Gracious	Respectful
Clever	Honest	Romantic
Compassionate	Honorable	Spontaneous
Confident	Humble	Sensitive
Considerate	Humorous	Sweet
Cooperative	Imaginative	Trustworthy
Courageous	Innovative	Venturesome
Creative	Intuitive	Warm
Dedicated	Kind	Wise
Dignified	Leader	Witty
Eloquent	Logical	Youthful
Enthusiastic	Lovable	Zealous

You may decide that you want to be like John Doe because he is successful. Reverse engineering the characteristics and thinking of success will help you identify what characteristics and thinking you want to "put on". If you adopt the characteristics that you believe make up success, those inner characteristics will result in your outer experience of success. What are some of the characteristics of success? Maybe successful characteristics include confidence, courage, creativity, dedication, focus, generosity, honesty, innovation, resourcefulness, and trustworthiness.

If there is an outer experience that you would like to achieve such as success or leadership, all you have to do is figure out the characteristics and corresponding thinking that you believe go into that outcome and "put them on" as we will discuss. As you "put on" the characteristics of the person you want to be, and persist in that way of thinking and being, you will become that new person. Repetition. Repetition. Repetition. New thoughts literally rewire your brain architecture.

The person that you are "being" or experiencing today is an exact result of your thinking up to now. In every moment, you will "be" someone. You can either intentionally "put on" the person that you want to be, or unintentionally default to the person you probably don't want to be as a result of slopping thinking, slopping behavior and believing you are a victim of circumstance.

In other words, you are the person that is playing in your mind, whether it is wanted or not. Get intentional about the person that you are "putting on" in your mind — and you will become that person.

2

START FROM THE END

What we call the beginning is often the end. And to make an end is to make a beginning. The end is where we start from.

— *T. S. Eliot*

Start with the end in mind in order to create what you want. If you don't know what you want to accomplish, you are extremely unlikely to get there. And, even if you did somehow miraculously get there, you would not realize you are "there" because you didn't know where you were headed. The first step is to figure out where "there" is.

You must have a clear outcome in mind so that you can apply these principles to achieve it. Some people have never considered the fact that they can actually achieve the outcome that they want so they really haven't given any thought to where "there" would be. Most people tend to believe that life "just happens". They believe that they have very little control of their life experience, and for the most part, they are the "victim of circumstances". Nothing could be further from the truth. You are not the victim of circumstances. You are quite literally the creator of your circumstances.

I'm not going to take you on an exotic journey of science or metaphysics to prove my point, although the science does exist. I'm going to show you very practically how this is true in your daily life. In order to receive a benefit from this book, be receptive to the idea that "you are the creator of your life experience." At a minimum, you agree that you are the creator of how you experience life. If this is true, and hopefully by the end of the book you will believe me, then what would you like to experience?

Really, please give this consideration. Once you know who you want to be, and the life experience you would like to have, then the next step is to create a Virtual Vision.

To Create a Virtual Vision

Identify who you want to be?

What are the characteristics of this person?

What would be happening in your life
if you were this person?

What would be the specific scene that is occurring?

What do you see?

How does it feel?

How does it smell?

How does it taste?

What are the sounds associated with this scene?

What are all the tactile sensory experiences
in this scenario?

Now, write a highly descriptive or Virtual Vision from the end result *as though it has already occurred*. (Be sure not to include "how" you got there). Use highly descriptive words engaging all the senses — sight, smell, taste, touch, and hearing.

I often say, write it like a romance novel. When you read an explicit romance novel, you are right in the scene in the moment feeling all the experiences of the characters. For example, "the tall, dark and handsome loner swept her up into his arms with a firm embrace and brushed his soft lips across her succulent neck." You get the idea, right? You are in the scene experiencing it. That is how to write an effective Virtual Vision using explicit, descriptive sensory detail.

This process can be used to shift the results in any area of your life. Often, people want to make changes in these primary areas, but by all means, be expansive and creative and add to this list:

Finances
Relationships
Health
Career

It may be easier for you to start with one area in order to "get the hang of it". Once you have some traction, you can add more components. Think of your Virtual Vision as a living document that you will continue to refine and enhance. As you accomplish the experiences in your Virtual Vision, you will want to continue to clarify, expand and elaborate on them. The next chapter will cover how to use and work with your Virtual Vision.

The reason that this actually works is that our thoughts are electric and our emotions are magnetic. Our thoughts and desires program the field that exists all around us to have the experience that you want, and your emotions are magnetic which draws them back to you. So, "feeling as if" you are the person in your Virtual Vision will literally draw it to you. You are a vibrational match to the experience you want to have. When your emotional state or the vibration of your being does not match your desire, you cannot draw it back to you. That is why you have to "feel as if" you are the person in your Virtual Vision. Then, you are in resonance with it and can draw it back to you in the form of life experience. (You can find out more about "the field" by reading Lynne McTaggart's book with the same title.)

The concept of a Vision is not a new one. Sources include The Bible, Neville Goddard, and Mary Morrissey.

3

OWN IT, LIVE IT, BE IT

Nothing endures but personal qualities.
— Walt Whitman

Whether you understand the science behind it or not, life has told you that there is something magical about making a decision. Often times, you think about doing something. You consider it. You contemplate it. You ruminate about it. And, of course, nothing happens. Sometimes you even "try" to do it. I always say, don't bother "trying" to do something. While you may make a little progress, you will exert significant effort with minimal gain. Trying to do something yields very minimal results. Never "try" to do anything. Either do it or don't do it. When you are actually ready to do it, make a decision and then you will be supporting yourself with the brain structure to carry it out.

When it comes to deciding who you want to be, after you've contemplated it and identified the characteristics of the person you want to be, make a decision to "put on" or "become" that person in thought, word, deed and character.

The magic of making a decision is what happens in your brain. When we actually "make a decision", three different parts of our brain fire simultaneously in order to reorganize neuro-pathways in our brain. This actually causes new architecture in your brain and allows you to think in a new way, which will support you in carrying out the decision that you have already made. If you are interested, you can do your own research on the relatively new field known as "decision neuroscience" which involves mapping thinking on a cellular level.

Now that you have actually "made a decision", you need to "put it on". In other words, you need to become it. You need to own it. You need to practice the thinking and feeling that supports the decision so frequently, regularly, continuously and habitually, it now becomes your new neurological network — your new way of being. With focus and repetition, you will become a new person. And, when this happens, you don't need to practice it any longer, you are now the person that you want to be naturally. It is now your "hard wiring".

Before you get to the point that it is your hardwiring, how do you "put it on"? In an earlier chapter, we talked about identifying the characteristics and thinking of the person that you want to become. Now you need to feel "as if" we have those characteristics. You are that person. You are living the experience in your Virtual Vision. How do those characteristics feel?

Let's say you have decided to be a confident, successful leader. Of course, you have developed the list of all the characteristics already. And, you have written a Virtual Vision outlining a scene as though it has already occurred. Take these characteristics and "feel as if" we are the person with those characteristics. For example, how does confidence feel? Confidence feels solid. Confidence feels like knowing. Confidence feels like inner peace. Confidence feels like knowing that you are fully capable of handling whatever comes up. Confidence feels like self-assurance. Confidence feels like flow. Confidence feels like ease. Confidence feels capable. Confidence is interested in what happens and fully capable of responding, engaging, interacting, sharing and being.

Consider all the characteristics of the person that you decided that you want to be. What are all the characteristics and then explore how they feel. Let's take another one. How does it feel to be innovative? Innovative feels capable. Innovative feels clever. Innovative feels creative. Innovative feels like a flow of endless ideas. Innovative feels energetic. Innovative feels expectant. Innovative feels hopeful. Innovative feels flexible. Innovative feels nimble.

You "put on" characteristics by feeling those characteristics literally in your body. Not just thinking about the components of the characteristics, but drawing them into your body — or really letting them well up from within your body — and feeling them as if you are actually having that experience right now.

You have had past experiences of feeling confident. A great technique is to recall a time that you felt that characteristic, recall the memory and re-experience it now. Put yourself back in that moment, in that scene, in that experience and feel how it felt to be confident. Really immerse yourself back into that experience so you can capture the feeling. As I said before, your feelings are magnetic and draw experiences to you. It is very important to feel feelings that match experiences that you want to have in your life. Recalling a prior time that you felt that emotion is one of the most effective ways of capturing the feeling again.

As an aside, you probably think that memories are related to time, but they are not. I'm going to prove it to you. Where were you on 9/11 when you heard of the tragic event? I bet you can recall exactly where you were, what you were doing, what you were wearing and whom you were with. Now, tell me what you were doing last Tuesday afternoon. Hmmm…. Unless it was somehow a special day or you had a specific activity scheduled, you are likely fuzzy on the details. 9/11 happened two decades ago and you are crystal clear on the details. Last Tuesday is less than a week ago and you cannot recall what you were doing. Your ability to recall does not relate to time, it relates to the emotional intensity of the event. (Thank you, Dr. Joe Dispenza).

Back to "putting on" the characteristics of the person you've decided to become. You can recall significant experiences in your life because of the heightened emotion involved in the experience. This gives you the tools to recapture the feelings of characteristics that you now want to "put on".

Feel the feelings of the person that you have decided to be. Feel the scenario that you have written in your Virtual Vision. Conjure up the virtual experience as though it is literally happening just as you have written it. You feel the environment or atmosphere as you have described it. You smell the fragrances that you have described. You feel the textures under your fingertips or on your skin as you have written them. You taste anything as though it is literally on your tongue. You are in fully immersed the scene. Of all the things that you can do to become the ideal person that you have identified, this is the key to actually becoming that person — feel "as if" you are that person right now having the experience.

Contrary to popular belief, it is not action that creates your results. It is "who you are being" as you take action. Doing action from the place of feeling "as if" you are the person that you've decided to be will yield super results, but it requires capturing the feeling first before any action is taken. Otherwise, you can actually be taking action in the direction away from who you want to become. Capture the feeling first!

This chapter is about making a decision and "putting it on". I'd like to take it one step further and say, "burn the ships". As the story goes, which you may have heard before, in 1519 Captain Hernan Cortez landed in Veracruz to begin his great conquest. Upon landing, he ordered his crew to "burn all the ships" that they had arrived on. As they were seriously outmanned, the captain wanted to ensure that retreat was not an option and they were truly, fully committed to winning the battle. Since the ability to retreat had been eliminated, the soldiers would win or die. They won.

In order to facilitate becoming the person you've decided to be, "burn the ships" and decide that no matter what, you will become that person. No matter what someone else thinks or says. No matter what other distractions or time commitments you have. No matter how long it takes. Of course, you are going to stumble. You are going to revert back to many of your old habits. But, if you have truly decided that it is worth it to become this new person, you will keep getting back on the proverbial bike and it will get easier and easier. Until one day, you are the person that you've identified you want to be and you cannot even imagine assuming the identity, characteristics or behavior of the old self. You have literally become a new person.

"I know it works because I've done it for myself. I used to be very angry and on edge all the time. I remember a few times thinking to myself "what am I angry about?" I had nothing. There was not an actual reason for my anger. My emotional set point was anger and it didn't take much to tip me over the edge. Now, after years of doing my own processing work, it would take something monumental to trigger anger in me. I cannot remember the last time I have been angry. It just isn't there anymore. Trust me, if I can do it, you can do it too!"

4

SELF AWARENESS & COURSE CORRECTION

If you don't like something, change it. If you can't change it, change your attitude.

— *Maya Angelou*

Now that you have made a decision, burned the ships, and learned how to "put on" your new thinking, you need to continuously be aware.

Huh? As you make the transition from the your old self to your new self, you need to be aware of who you are being in the moment so you can continue to course correct when you inevitably revert back to old thoughts and behavior.

In other words, during this transition process, you are often going to fall back into your old behavior, which is perfectly normal. You have been living as the old self your whole life up to this point. So, you need to be aware of when you are back in that old thinking/behavior so we can do a "course correction" to stop the old thinking.

As you are aware, and you notice that you are thinking like the old self... "I'm not worthy, it never works for me, life is hard" — Stop! As soon as you recognize this thinking, stop it! Do not continue the thought. Stop in the middle. In your own mind, you usually say, "as soon as I complete this thought," I'll stop thinking like this. Stop! You don't have to finish the thought. This breaks the pattern. Stop midstream. Have a "replacement" thought that you can substitute.

Develop a list of intentional thoughts that you can repeat over and over to begin developing new, positive thought patterns. You can use this list intentionally every day to build up traction on your new way of thinking. And, you can have this list ready to draw from when you find yourself in old thinking patterns. Here are some suggestions, but I want you to expand on this list for your own use.

> *Things always work out for me.*
>
> *This too shall pass.*
>
> *I have lots of skills and talent.*
>
> *Opportunities are always available.*
>
> *The sun is shining.*
>
> *I'm proud of myself for adopting a new way of thinking.*
>
> *I have lots of friends and support.*
>
> *I love the first cup of coffee in the morning.*
>
> *I'm alive.*
>
> *I love the smell of flowers.*
>
> *I love the way my dog licks my face.*
>
> *I've made a decision and I'm sticking to it.*
>
> *My heart is in the right place.*

I love rainbows, unicorns or flying monkeys…. (It doesn't even have to be logical. Just interrupt the negative thought pattern).

Adopting a new way of being requires continual awareness and correction to "put on" the new self. Set up systems and reminders to ensure that you remember to practice your new way of thinking.

Set Up Reminder Systems

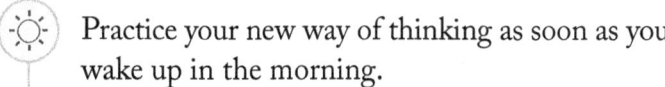

Practice your new way of thinking as soon as you wake up in the morning.

Make sure positive thoughts and/or your Virtual Vision are your last thoughts as you drift off to sleep. This is a very fertile and receptive time for your thoughts to drift into your subconscious so be vigilant about the thoughts you think before you go to sleep.

Set an hourly reminder to check in with your thinking. Think about what you've been thinking about.

Create touchstone that you experience multiple times per day that are a good reminder, like when you are driving, when you are eating, when you are going to the toilet. (Okay, that is unconventional, but you do it many times per day and it provides a great opportunity to check in with yourself.)

Ask friends to prompt you.

 Is there a reminder app. I bet there is…

If you want to "super-charge" your results, ask friends and family to lovingly hold you accountable to your new way of thinking. Whenever they notice you reverting back to your old thoughts and old behavior, they will probably be very happy to point it out to you. It is a win-win for all concerned. And, who knows, maybe they will upgrade their thinking too!

5

YOU ARE THE AUTHOR OF YOUR STORY—TELL A NEW ONE

There is a world of difference between truth and facts. Facts can obscure the truth.

— *Maya Angelou*

As I explained, you are the product of your thinking. The life you are living right now is an exact match for the quality and content of your thinking. In other words, you are a product of the story that you tell about yourself, and most importantly, *to* yourself. I know. I know. This is very hard to believe. You think you are a "victim of circumstances". No, you are the creator of circumstances. At a minimum, you are the experiencer of circumstances according to the story you tell. And then, you experience the circumstances and tell a story about those circumstances according to the way you perceive them. Moreover, you keep telling the same old story, which reinforces the state of mind that matches the experience.

My infamous fishing story that explains how this work. This isn't about the "big one" that got way. Here is how the fishing story got started. I was riding along in the car with my niece's son, Adrian. I was explaining to him how perception works. My explanation was somewhat theoretical. Adrian asked for a real life example to make it easier to understand. Great, "give me a topic and I will show you how this works." Adrian, being an avid fisherman himself, said "fishing." Perfect.

One guy loves everything about fishing. He loves getting up early in the morning. He feels like he is getting a great start to the day. He loves being out in nature. He loves the tranquility and beauty of nature. He loves seeing the animals scamper around. Of course, he loves the excitement of catching a fish. He loves eating fish. This guy loves fishing.

Much to Adrian's dismay, the next guy hates fishing. He hates getting up early. He hates getting out in nature. It is too quiet. It is boring. It is often cold. He is afraid that he might be eaten by a bear. He hates putting the worm on the hook. He hates waiting to see if a fish is going to bite. This guy hates everything about fishing.

Fishing is neutral. Fishing has no meaning at all. Fishing only has the meaning that you give it. Fishing is a neutral experience. You are giving it all the meaning that you experience by the story you tell about it. And, absolutely everything is like that whether it be school, a job, a relationship, anything at all. In fact, you don't experience the "thing" you are talking about. You experience your perception about the thing you are talking about. And, you can see that this is true because you can love fishing or hate fishing. What you are experiencing are your thoughts, your emotions and your perspective about it. When it comes to fishing, no big deal. You can love it or hate it. But, when it comes to other areas of your life, you may want to tell a new story.

On a related subject to show you that you don't experience "the thing", you experience your thoughts about the thing, let's explore the placebo effect. In Dr. Joe Dispenza's book titled *You Are The Placebo*, he gives many examples of people experiencing an outcome based on their expectations irrespective of the facts. This proves that you do not experience "the thing". You experience your thoughts "about the thing". Here are a couple paraphrased examples from his book.

In 1996, orthopedic surgeon Bruce Moseley with Baylor College of Medicine published a trial study based on the experience with ten volunteers, all of whom had suffered from osteoarthritis of the knee. Two of the men receive a standard surgery called debridement. Three of the men received a lavage procedure. Five of the men received a "pretend" or placebo surgery in which an incision was made so it appeared that a surgery was done, but no actual procedure occurred. A screen was used to shield the patient from the surgeon pretending to do the surgery and a video was shown on a television screen making the patient believe that it was an actual surgery. The patient truly believed that he received a surgery, which was key to making it work.

After the surgery, all ten of the patients reported greater mobility and less pain. In fact, the men who received "pretend" surgeries did just as well as those who receive an actual surgery. Furthermore, the results continued to hold true for months and even years after the study.

Another study in the late 1950's cited by Dr. Dispenza involved heart surgery. This study featured two groups of researchers at Kansas City and Seattle. At each location, their patient pool was divided into two groups. One group received the standard internal mammary ligation and the second group received a "pretend" surgery. (The surgeon made a small incision in the patients' chests and acted as if the surgery occurred, and then sewed up the patient. The patients were convinced that they received a real surgery).

The results at each location were very similar: 67 percent of the patients who received the actual surgery felt less pain and needed less medication, while 83 percent of the "pretend" surgeries experienced improvement. In other words, the pretend surgeries actually achieved better results.

These are only two of numerous cases demonstrating the placebo affect. Because the patient believed that they received the actual procedure and believed they would improve, they did. In other words, they believed the story that they were telling themselves and so they had the matching outcome. There were other stories cited using the principle in reverse, such as a man freezing to death in a train boxcar because he believed that the refrigeration was on. It was not. He froze to death in temperatures well above 32 degrees because of his thoughts, not the temperature.

Now, I want to look at the idea of the story we tell ourselves according to the "labels" we use. Since birth, you learned the "label" or "name" that you call everything. This is a ball. This is a car. This is red. This is a flower. This is a cup of tea. Literally, everything that you experience, see, touch, taste or smell has a label. And, because you have experienced these items in the past, you often do not experience "the thing" itself. You experience your relationship with the label.

You know what a cup of tea is going to taste like, so you expect that taste even before you take the first sip. (Have you every experienced your mouth curling up when you took a sip of something because you expected it to be a different drink?) You have a pre-programmed perception or story for everything. And, that has many benefits for you in organizing the barrage of data that is constantly coming at you. But, it can also have a very negative affect. If one time, you had a negative experience with something (say eating fish that was "off"), you now can no longer eat fish because you have a preprogrammed experience subconsciously that gets triggered when you think of that subject. Your stomach will literally turn at the thought. Again, you are not experiencing "the thing". You are experiencing your story about the thing.

This also explains why people love having first time experiences so much. You look forward to your first kiss. Some people look forward to skydiving for the first time. Or, any experience that you have never had before. Why? You don't have any preprogrammed data or story in our mind about it. You are actually going to experience **the real thing for the first time** — rather than any pre-programmed story.

How does this tie to the chapter title, "You are the Author of Your Story, Tell a New One"? Most of the time, you are not experiencing life. You are experiencing your pre-programmed expectations and labels about life. Or, you are re-experiencing a pattern that you have wired in your brain. When you ask, how did you "re-act"? What you are really saying is, how did you re-experience an act that you've already had rather than experience it this time according to the actual event or circumstance.

If you do not like how you are experiencing life (a.k.a. you don't enjoy the fishing trip you are on), you need to tell a new story about it. You will experience the story according to your thoughts, beliefs, and expectations. You can stop a story mid-stream and decide to tell a new one. You can take the same "facts" that occurred and tell a new story with them.

Let's look at an example. Here are some facts: abandoned, unhealthy, and no money. One person can tell the story that because he was an unhealthy child, he was abandoned, had no support, grew up with no money and now he is doomed to be on welfare because he had no opportunities. He is a victim of his circumstances.

Another person may have been unhealthy at birth, grown up in an orphanage and seemed to have no money and no opportunities, and taken those same life circumstances to propel themselves to be self sufficient, independent, street smart, Sauvé and capable. Using all those skills, they made opportunities for themselves and succeeded beyond anyone's wildest expectations. J. K. Rowling and Oprah Winfrey are great examples of starting with meager beginnings.

You are not a victim of circumstances. You are a "victim" or "benefactor" of what you tell yourselves about your circumstances. You can take where you are right now and use everything you've ever learned to tell a story of accomplishment and success. Once you tell a success story and literally "put it on" and be it, you will create the outer experience to match it.

6

THE GENIUS OF EMOTIONS

Follow your instincts.
That's where true wisdom manifests itself.

— *Oprah Winfrey*

Fortunately, everyone comes full equipped with a genius feedback system to tell you if your life is on track or off track — your emotions! Your emotions are the most accurate and sophisticated guidance system that you could ever have, if you understand them and pay attention to them. Unfortunately, many people often think of emotions as unnecessary or irrational and push them aside.

This creates a host or problems in itself as you can never really "get rid of" your emotions. You can only suppress them or cover them up with food, alcohol, drugs, sex, shopping, work or some other Band-Aid. And, then you still have to deal with both the original problem and the repercussions of whatever you have been doing to suppress and avoid the feelings that you have been covering up.

While you may not realize it, you are always experiencing an emotion or an emotional state 24/7/365. Now, some of you may say, "no, not me." I'm not emotional. Not true. You are always experiencing an emotional state. You tend to only recognize emotions that are very high (like bliss or joy), very low emotions (like depression, sadness or grief) or very strong emotions (like anger or fear). But, you always exist in an emotional state. Your emotions may be calm, focused, peaceful, or bored so they don't get your attention, but you cannot exist without being in an underlying emotional state.

Your thoughts trigger your emotions continuously. Here is how it works. You have a thought, and it triggers a corresponding emotion. For example, if you have thoughts like "someone is going to get you," you will trigger anxiety or fear depending on the intensity of your thought.

Your general way of thinking, the culmination of all the over 60,000 thoughts you have each day, creates an "emotional set point". Everyone has an emotional set point. It is sort of the "way you feel" when you get up in the morning. The important thing to know is that you can shift your emotional set point if it is not bringing you the results and experiences that you desire. Even if you are experiencing a generally positive emotional set point and a good life, you can still elevate your emotional set point to create an even better life experience.

Your emotions or emotional set point actually determines how you experience life. From a physics standpoint, it not only attracts the experiences that you call to yourself in life, it also determines the filter with which you interpret or perceive your life. In other words, it takes the facts and runs them through the "story" you tell yourself about the facts to create how you perceive or experience your life.

You cannot look out from the emotional set point of worry and see a happy, carefree world. If you are worried, you can only look out from that perspective and see things that validate that this is a treacherous world with many things that you should be afraid of.

Conversely, you cannot be at the emotional set point of joy and look out and see a world of strife and fear. You will see the world in the corresponding way that matches your emotional set point. The real magic is to change your emotional set point, which will change how you experience your life and the world you see. And, quite literally, this will actually draw to you experiences that match your emotions based on the law of resonance.

Your emotions are absolutely integral to your health and well-being. Your emotions actually determine the rhythm of your heartbeat on a beat-by-beat basis. According to HeartMath Institute, when you are feeling positive emotions such as joy or happiness, your heart beats in a "coherent" (ordered, organized) rhythm. Conversely, when you are upset, irritated, angry, sad or any other depleting emotion, it causes your heart to beat in an "incoherent", (disorganized, erratic and chaotic) rhythm. The shape of your heart rhythm is fundamental to your health. The Bible says, "a merry heart is like a medicine." It turns out this is literally true based on science.

Your heart rhythm, either coherent or incoherent, determines how your Autonomic Nervous System (ANS) works. When your heart is coherent and organized, your ANS is flowing in balance and in an optimal state. When your heart rhythm is incoherent and chaotic, the two branches of your ANS are not working in harmony. The sympathetic branch of the ANS is designed to speed up your heart rhythm. The parasympathetic branch is designed to slow your heart down. When your heart is incoherent, it is like having one foot on the gas and one foot on the brake at the same time. What does this do to your automobile? It creates a lot of wear and tear on your vehicle, poor gas mileage and ultimately it will reduce the useful life of the vehicle. This "stress" on your ANS has the same affect on your physical vehicle. And, it all starts with your emotions — or more precisely, the thoughts you think to trigger your emotions.

How your ANS works at any moment also affects the way your brain functions. When your heart is coherent, your ANS is in balance and the impulses from your heart to the brain reach the frontal lobe where your "executive functions" like creativity, reasoning, problem solving and intuition reside. When your ANS is out of balance and chaotic, the impulses that go from your heart to your brain go to the reptilian part of your brain where "fight or flight" reside. This is also where you get into "repeating patterns". Again, how did you re-act? How did you do an act again that you have done over and over again? Literally, when you are upset, you cannot get out of the old thought/behavior loop.

When you experience negative emotions, it causes a chain reaction. Your heart rhythm becomes incoherent, your ANS goes out of balance and the impulses from your heart to your brain go to the reptilian part of the brain. This causes you to repeat negative behavior that you say that you are going to stop. And, when you say that you are going to stop doing it, you mean it. But, if the impulses are in the reptil-ian part of the brain, this is the only behavior that you can access at that moment.

The genius of your feelings is that they provide the perfect feedback to tell you which dynamic you are experiencing. You are either experiencing positive emotions that mean that your heart is coherent, your ANS is working properly and your brain is accessing the frontal lobe. Or, you are expe-riencing negative emotions that tell us your heart rhythm is incoherent, your ANS it out of balance and you are in the reptilian part of the brain. Your emotions are feedback!

According to HMI, emotions also determine which set of hormones and chemicals get released into your system in any moment. When you are experiencing positive thoughts that trigger positive emotions, you release over 1,400 hormones and chemicals including DHEA which is known as the "vitality" hormone. This has a host of positive affects like improved memory, increased muscle mass, and increased longevity.

When you are experiencing negative emotions, you also release over 1,400 hormones and chemicals into your body. The primary hormone that you release when you are experiencing negative emotions is cortisol, also known as the stress hormone. Cortisol is linked to memory loss, reduced muscle mass and accelerated aging and a host of other negative consequences.

Emotions serve as feedback to tell us where our thoughts have been. Every emotion will lead you right back to the corresponding quality of thought that matches the emotion. As outlined in Dr. David Hawkins book *Power vs. Force*, below are some excerpts of the numeric value placed on various emotions:

Peace	600
Love	500
Reason	400
Acceptance	350
Neutrality	250
Courage	200
Anger	150
Fear	100
Grief	75
Guilt	30
Shame	20

Every emotion has a quantifiable number and more importantly "state". Every emotion has a corresponding "state of being". Every emotion has corresponding types of behavior. It is important to move up the emotional scale to a higher "state of being" so you can improve the quality of your behavior and life experience.

In any moment, you may be in a negative emotion. It is important that you don't just look at the emotion itself, but where you have come from. For example, if you were in a state of guilt and are now in anger, you are actually moving up the emotional scale to a more positive state. On the other hand, if you were in acceptance and have move to anger, you are now moving down the emotional scale. Anger may be going in the right direction or the wrong direction, depending on where you are coming from. You just don't want to hang out there. You want to move up to neutrality and beyond so you can begin to experience the positive dynamics of a coherent heart rhythm and all the benefits it provides.

Another way to use emotions as feedback is to feel how much "resistance" you are experiencing. You cannot be in a high emotional state and also have the presence of resistance. In fact, it is the absence of resistance that will result in you moving up the emotional scale to a higher state of being.

There is a natural flow to your life. There is a natural ease. All things should be flowing well and things coming to you easily and in order. When you have doubt, fear, worry or anger, it is like a block or a crimp on the flow. It feels forced, tight and constricted and inhibits the flow. Resistance stops you from being able to access the high quality emotions, which have a corresponding high quality experience. These high quality experiences are your natural birthright when you drop resistance.

Here is one of the best analogize that I have come up with that helps you to understand your natural state, operating without resistance.

Think of the Internet. The Internet is always there. It is always available. Sometimes you are connected to it. Sometimes you are not connected to it. Whether you are connected to it or not doesn't determine whether it is there or not. It is there and you may or may not be connected to it in the moment. When you get "triggered" and are in a negative emotional state, you experience "resistance" and you are now disconnected from your Internet connection. That doesn't mean that the Internet has gone away. It just means that you've lost your connection. In this analogy, you cannot reconnect until you drop the resistance and get back into a positive emotion, which results in connection.

Really, there are only two types of emotions with endless variations of them: Love and fear. You may call them all kinds of different names, but there are those feels that integrate you, build you up, unite you which I call Love. And, there are those emotions that disintegrate you, tear you down, disconnect you, which are all versions of fear.

Love unites you. Love allows you to flow. Love allows you to be connected. Love is a very high emotional state and you will receive all the corresponding physical, mental and emotional benefits from being in this high emotional state.

Conversely, fear and anger and all the other negative emotions disconnect you, which causes you to get into an incoherent heart rhythm, throws your ANS out of balance, gets you into the reptilian part of the brain, causes you to release cortisol in your system and all the other adverse affects you experience. In other words, fear causes you to get disconnected from the Internet.

Choose Love.

7

EMOTIONS DIRECT COMMUNICATIONS

Who you are speaks so loudly
I can't hear what you're saying.

— Ralph Waldo Emerson

You may be surprised to learn that your emotions actually affect other people and the surrounding environment. If you stop to think about it, you intuitively know this is true. Have you ever gone into a room and even though nobody is talking, you feel that you could "cut the tension with a knife"?

You also know that being around certain people elevates your mood and feels uplifting, while spending time around other people "sucks the life out of you". This is due to the energetics of emotions.

According to HeartMath Institute, our heart is electric and wherever there is electricity, a magnetic field is created. This is basic physics. So, we have an electromagnetic field around our body extending out three feet in every direction. Actually, it is believed to be much larger, but currently the instrumentation needed to measure it does not exist. We communicate through this electromagnetic field. HMI has done many studies on the affect of our emotions on other people. Here are a couple summarized examples.

In one study, a boy and his dog went into the laboratory both wearing heart rate monitors. The dog had never been allowed into the laboratory so she was sniffing around and exploring. The boy was asked to shift into a coherent heart rhythm and send love and care to his dog. When he did so, the boy and the dog's heart rhythm became coherent and went into sync.

In another experiment involved a mother and her baby using a technique called signal averaging measured the energetic exchange between them. In this experiment, the mother was not touching or engaging with her baby. When she focused her thoughts on her baby, her brainwaves and the baby's heartbeat went into sync.

HMI also conducted a group experiment involving forty participants. Thirty of the participants were training in a technique that allowed them to become "heart coherent". The other ten people were control subjects. In the experiment, the participants were put into ten groups of four participants, all wearing heart rate monitors. At a particular point, the thirty trained participants became heart coherent. The ten control subjects were unaware. However, when the three participants in each group got coherent, the fourth participant switched into a state of coherence simply based on the coherent field environment affect of the other participants. In other words, the emotional state of the three people caused the forth person to become coherent.

In reality, you make an energetic imprint on the environment. Imagine yourself emitting your thoughts and emotions into the environment, which are picked up by other people. It is as thought you leave an energetic trail behind you. You create an "atmosphere" or vibrational environment around yourself. And, of course, you pick up the energetic imprint of other people as well. In fact, you often react to it at a cellular level, even though you don't understand why.

Mastering your thoughts, which allows you to master your emotional state is the key to "being your most influential self in any situation". The person who is coherent rules the energy exchange in any interaction. When you become coherent, you provide a wonderful benefit to other people in your environment making it easier for them to get coherent themselves.

In spiritual circles, I've often heard the phrase that someone is "holding the space" for another person. The coherent field environment explains this dynamic.

8

DECODING THE PROCESS

All action results from thought, so it is thoughts that matter.
— *Sai Baba*

People tend to believe that thoughts are not "real things". Therefore, they have no real affect. Laboratory research has demonstrated the ability to actually measure the frequency and geometry of a thought. In fact, with an 80% accuracy rating, the researcher can determine the thought someone is thinking by analyzing the readout. Thoughts are real and primary to the experiences you have in life. In the Bible, it states, "as a man thinketh in his heart, so is he." This has been scientifically validated.

Positive affirmations don't work. Huh? I've just said that thought is primary and the quality of your thought determines the emotional state you experience, so positive affirmations should work. Right? Well, they would if you believed them. Of course, if you believed them, you wouldn't need positive affirmations, you would be having the matching experience.

In other words, you cannot simply make positive affirmations that you don't believe and achieve a corresponding result. The outcome matches your vibration, not your words.

If you don't believe words you are saying, you are in a state of "lack", no matter what words you are saying. From an energetic standpoint, you are actually projecting the opposite. You have to make affirmations that you believe.

One method that does work is to walk yourself up the emotional scale using statements or affirmation that you do believe to gradually increase your emotional vibration. So, for example, if you are experiencing financial problems, it won't work to say "I'm rich. I'm rich." But, what will make an internal shift is to say things that you do believe, such as, "things always turn out okay," "I have plenty of options," "I have enough money to take care of my bills right now" and "I have a lot of skills that are in demand." In walking yourself up the emotional scale, you start from where you truly are and build up to a higher quality thought. You must be in "integrity". Integrity is integration: your thoughts, words and vibration are in alignment.

Another important reminder is to focus on what you want rather than dwelling on what you don't want. Or, focus on the solution rather than continuing to focus on the problem. So often, people focus on a problem and expect a solution to appear. The vibration of a problem is vastly different than the vibration of a solution. You cannot focus on a low vibration problem and expect a high vibration solution. You must let go of the energy of the problem by shifting your focus away from it. This allows a solution to become apparent.

The perfect example of this concept is when Mother Teresa was asked to attend an anti-war rally. Wisely, she declined and said that she wouldn't attend an anti-war rally, but if they had a pro-peace event, she would be glad to participate. She knew to focus on what she wanted (peace) rather than fight against what she didn't want (war). Fighting against what you don't want is sure to keep it in place as you are adding all your thought, focus and energy to it.

While thought is primary, the process goes deeper. Not only do you have thoughts, but also "thought patterns". You pick up these patterns or programming when you are a small child by observing, experiencing and feeling how your primary authority figures deal with life. Dr. Michael Ryce calls this the "power person" dynamic. Your power person is the person in your life that has the most authority and influence over you when you are a small child in your formative years.

When you are a young child, you learn to get along with your power person and navigate life with them. When the stress is up, you also learn how to resist your power person. Unchecked when you get older, you now subconsciously operate your life through this same power person dynamic with other people in your life.

When life is going along okay, you tend to interact with others in the way that you interacted with your power person. When stress increases, you tend to resist other people in some form that is similar to how you resisted your power person. Then, under extreme stress, you assume a version of the behavior you disliked the most about your power person. And, of course, this all goes on below your conscious awareness.

This dynamic is easy to identify when it is very prominent,

such as a domestic violence pattern. Subtle patterns, particularly related to money, relationships and health, are also picked up in your impressionable, formative years. Research claims that over 80% of your programming is established by eight years old.

These patterns or programming are passed from generation to generation. The Bible says, "the sins of our fathers will be passed down to the third and fourth generation." A modern translation is thought and behavior patterns and programming are passed from generation to generation which result in behavior dynamics.

I believe it is much easier to understand this dynamic with a real life example so here is my personal story.

As a child, I lived in Australia with my parents and two older sisters. My parents decided to get divorced and my mother, my two sisters and I moved back to the United States. This was in the late 70's. At that time, there was no Internet, Skype or video chat apps, international calls were over $3 per minute and flying across the globe was prohibitively expensive. As a result, I did not see my father very often. While I was unaware of the impact this was having on me at the time, I developed an abandonment pattern. And, as life would have it, if you have a thought pattern, even if it is at a subconscious level, you will live it out until you change the architecture of your thinking.

So, as I become older, I found myself in relationships with men who always seem to abandon me in some fashion. This happened many times before I realized that I was the common denominator and began working on my own programming. After doing a lot of work on my own patterns, I had a major revelation. This is also a family generational pattern.

My father was the middle child of five children. For whatever reason, his mother decided that she did not want to raise him, although she raised all of her other children. She shipped my dad off to grandma. Consequently, he developed an abandonment pattern.

My grandfather and his family moved to the United States from Ireland when he was two years old. When he was four years old, his father went out to get milk. He still hasn't returned. Of course, my grandfather had an abandonment pattern.

This was all very interesting, but the dagger to my heart was when I looked at my oldest son's patterns. My oldest son lived with me until he was 18. He was well taken care of and had anything he could need or want. How in the world would he have an abandonment issue? Well, in those years, I was a Corporate Vice President for a multi-billion dollar, publicly traded company in a very unusual environment. The CEO of the company, my boss, was quadriplegic and had a sleep disorder. Due to these circumstances, he often worked twenty plus hours per day. He liked to work all night long and get just a few hours sleep in the morning. This meant that I worked several nights per week all night long, and got very little sleep. When I wasn't working, I was "on call" and he called often for hours on end and almost every Sunday night. So, even though my son and I lived in the same house, he felt abandoned by me. Yikes! The generational pattern became very clear to me.

As Dr. Joe Dispenza says, "thoughts that fire together, wire together" and create neurological pathways in your brain. You are living with the architecture of your thoughts. The only real way to transform thought patterns is to unwire those thoughts and re-wire them, or to override them and basically dissolve this architecture and re-establish new thought architecture. (I have several processes for this that are not outlined in this booklet as it requires dialogue).

It is also important to understand that you own your thinking. Nobody else does. I've heard "you make me angry" so many times. Actually, that is not true and it is not even possible. Nobody can "make" you angry, although they can "trigger" your anger. You may be saying, "so what." The "so what" is the difference between your ability to master your thinking, or trapped as a victim never to be able to run your own life.

Let me explain. Let's say, you and I and two other people are enjoying a meal at a restaurant. Someone comes into the restaurant and over to our table. This person begins yelling and screaming at us. If one person in our group gets angry, and another person becomes afraid, and the third person gets embarrassed and the fourth person just starts laughing, clearly what the intruder did didn't "make" anyone angry. If what he did "made" us get angry, we would all get angry. So, he didn't make us do anything. He triggered our most prominent thought pattern response to that type of stimuli. This goes hand-in-hand with the idea that you perceive through your own reality. Just like fishing, you see situations according to the "wiring" that you already have in place regarding a similar type of scenario. You don't see events as they happen. You see events according to your patterns and programming. You see events through your filters.

TURN UP YOUR
THERMOSTAT

It takes courage to grow up and become who you are.
— E.E. Cummings

As we've discussed, you have an internal thermostat or emotional set point. You experience life according to where your thermostat dial is set. The good news is that you can turn the thermostat up and create a more meaningful life whenever you decide.

Here is how your thermostat works. Everything is energy. Huh? Is that some new age concept? No. Food converts to energy. You need to eat food to have energy. Sleep restores your energy. If you've every had a four year old asking you continual questions, you may suggest, "go outside, run around and burn off some energy." When you stop to think about it, you know that you are an energy system. How you manage your energy system will determine where your internal thermostat is set.

Everything is energy. As I said before, there are only two types of energy, even though they have lots of different terms. Here are a few of those names: integrated and dis-integrated; Love and fear; coherence and incoherence. In other words, one type of energy builds up your system and the other type of energy tears down your system.

With that understanding, you obviously want to set your emotional set point on a high level. How do we do that? Truly, a high emotional set point is your natural state if you didn't have a lot of interference preventing you from experiencing yourselves in this state. In order to achieve that high set point, you need to remove interference or resistance. Resistance is any form of negative thought, negative thought patterns or negative believes that you hold against yourself or others.

You may feel that you are unworthy, untalented, unattractive or some other self-imposed limiting label. You may also hold these beliefs about other people like "he isn't fair to me," or "everybody picks on me." When you have negative thoughts about other people, or are judging them, you are actually putting that disintegrative energy into your system. If you think angry thoughts about them, you are literally dosing yourself with the low frequency energy of anger and causing yourself to become incoherent. To judge another is to harm yourself.

In addition to harming yourself when you judge another, I want to point out that what you see in another is truly about you. If you have a negative perception about someone else, this is entirely about your perspective or belief system (your fishing story) and not about them. If there is a particular "thing" you notice in a lot of people, like controlling behavior, you really need to look at yourself. This is really about you. These types of thoughts create interference or resistance in your energy system that would otherwise be at a high level if you were not pulling it down with these low quality thoughts.

Here is a list of ideas you can use to raise your emotional set point:

o Be in a state of Love. Love others without conditions or requirements. I occasionally say to one of my sons, "I love you, but I don't like your behavior." Remember that people are not their behavior so you can love them without agreeing with their actions. (Nobody is their behavior. They do behavior. Anything that can change is not who you really are.)

o Of all the attributes about something, focus only on the good ones.

o Be in a continual state of gratitude. You can only experience one emotion at a time. When you experience gratitude, you are not experiencing an emotion that drags you down.

o Focus on your successes.

o Do breathing techniques. When you are upset, you will notice that your breathing becomes shallow. A good way to get out of negative thoughts is to focus on your breathing and take slow, long, intentional breaths.

o Use the same facts to tell a new story. There truly is a silver lining in almost every situation. Even from so called bad situations, you learn many life skills. You may learn how to be resilient or how to be independent. Tell your story from the most beneficial standpoint.

○ Realize that you are experiencing your perception, which is not really true if someone else could have a different perception about the same event. This allows you to loosen up your grip on that perception and know that it is not really true.

○ Recognize in some situations you can choose to be right or choose to be happy. Choose to be happy. No body even remembers who was right tomorrow.

○ Take the "high road". While you may seem to miss a momentary satisfaction, the high road feels good and the benefits are lasting. (The low road has many adverse side affects).

○ Body language does actually affect your mood. Sit up straight. Stand up straight. Strike a power pose. You can do it!

○ Do activities that "trigger" you into feeling good like playing with your dog.

○ Listen to music that "triggers" positive emotions.

○ Whatever you are trying to avoid, instead really "feel it." When you don't resist things and fully experience them, surprisingly, they dissolve and fade away quickly.

- Slow down.

- Be in the present moment and really experience it. Engage your senses and live the moment.

- Go into the silence.

- Talk with a smile. The other person will feel it energetically.

- Walk yourself up the emotional scale by telling a better story that you truly believe. Things do always work out.... I have talent.... I am capable....

- Spend more time around people that feel good to you.

- Spend time doing a hobby that you enjoy.

The list of things that you can do to increase your emotional set point and bring you to a higher frequency is endless. Create your own list. Most importantly, do the things on the list. All of this is just a nice theory unless you implement it for yourself.

10

SKIP THE PROCESS;
GO DIRECTLY TO YOUR "WHY"

Love will find its way through all language on its own.
                                    — *Ralph Waldo Emerson*

I briefly mentioned thinking about your "why" earlier to give yourself motivation to keep "putting on" your new behavior. I want to elaborate on your "why" a little bit more here. What you think is your "why" probably is not.

From a traditional standpoint, you may have lots of "whys." Your "why's" may include:

> To earn more money.
> To feel secure.
> To purchase a big house.
> To drive a sports car.
> To get promoted.
> To find a spouse.
> To earn an award or recognition.
> To "one-up" another person.

I want you to know that none of the reasons listed above are your "why." In fact, you have only one real "why" and it is the same as everyone else's "why." Everything you do is for

Love. What? I am making the bold statement that everything that you do is for Love. Allow me to explain.

Why do you want a big house? You might say just because you like it and there may be some truth to that. But, often you want a big house so you can "keep up with the Jones." Why do you want to "keep up with the Jones"? So, they will respect you. Why do you want them to respect you? So they will like you. Why do you want them to like you? Because you want to feel like their equal. Why do you want to feel like their equal? So, you will feel Love. You are using the "big house" as a permission slip to feel Love.

Why do you want the promotion and big raise? So, you will be recognized and valued. Why do you want to be recognized and valued? So you will be accepted. Why do you want to be accepted? So, you will feel Loved. You may think this Love is coming from them, but it is actually coming from you. So you will approve of yourself and feel your own Love. The promotion and raise is about being accepted and Loved. It is your permission slip or touch stone to approve of and Love yourself.

Why do you want to "one-up" someone? So, you will feel superior. Why do you want to feel superior? So, you will be admired? Why do you want to be admired? So you will be approved of. In other words, so "they," and more importantly, "you," will Love you. You get the idea.

All of the "things" that you want to get, achieve, earn or acquire are for the same reason after you strip away the purposes that you believe they have. They are somehow a

60

symbol that you believe will allow you to get what you really want, which is to be accepted and Loved.

Skip the process (the house, the car, the trophy) and go directly to Love. When you Love and appreciate others, you are experiencing that emotion directly within yourself. Most likely, the other person will also return it to you. But, whether they do or not, you cannot control. What you can control is feeling the Love first within yourself.

When you can truly Love yourself irrespective of circumstances, you will not need Love from anyone else. Although, the law of resonance will surely bring it to you. You get a match for the state you are in. If you are in a state of Love, it will be coming from every direction. You will not need any "permission" slips or false idols to trigger you into that state.

Remember, your real "why" starts with Love.

11

LEAD FROM WHERE YOU ARE

The key to successful leadership today is influence, not authority.

— *Ken Blanchard*

It is imperative to understand that wherever you are is the perfect place. It doesn't matter what your life experience has been, your job position, your economic situation, your social status, your race, your religion or lack thereof, your creed or anything else. You are in the perfect place. You have complete control, power and dominion over your life no matter where you are. You have the power to think whatever you want to think, to believe whatever you want to believe, to perceive life according to the story you want to tell. You have everything you need in this moment to be your most influential self.

Assume complete responsibility for your life right now, no matter what your life experience is or has been. If you are incarcerated, that doesn't matter. You are still in control of your life because you are in control of your thinking. You might not have physical freedom. But, you have mental freedom to think whatever you want.

The only way to be truly joyful is to truly be fully in command of you. This means nobody "makes" you do anything. Again, if you are incarcerated, someone may make you do a physical activity. But, nobody makes you think about it in any way. You decide how you are going to think and what you are going to think. You own you!

There is a saying "what someone else thinks of you is none of your business." And this is true. What they think about you is about their thought patterns, their stories, their beliefs, and their perceptions. On the other hand, what you think about anyone else is really about you. If for any reason you don't like someone else, here is your opportunity to look in the mirror and ask yourself what are you thinking that causes this reaction. It is truly about your thinking and has nothing to do with them (even if they are a "rascal"). As you've already learned, you will receive the complete physical, mental, emotional, neurological, hormonal affect of your thinking so judging someone else is a condemnation on yourself.

In the Babemba tribe of South Africa, when a person acts irresponsibly or unjustly, he is placed in the middle of the village. All work stops, and every person in the village gathers in a large circle around the individual. Each tribal member recites the good things the person in the circle has done in his lifetime. All his positive attributes, good deeds, strengths, and kindnesses are recited at length often taking several days. At the end, a celebration is held welcoming the person back into the tribe. Whether they know it or not, they are using all the principles of how their emotions affect other people and program the environment to restore this person to his highest state. Imagine if we adopted this type of approach when someone has stepped out of his or her highest state or chosen less than loving behavior.

If you think about it, when someone is in a negative state of mind or doing disconnected behavior, what he or she needs most from you is Love. He is already getting plenty of disintegrative energy from his own negative thinking.

A Course In Miracles states, "anger is never justified." First, anger is not justified because "you are doing it to yourself" energetically and emotionally. And, second, knowing that whatever emotion you are holding either helps to bring up the other person or tear them down energetically. No matter what they have done, it is never going to be helpful to you, them or anyone else to experience your negatively charged emotional environment.

Great leaders actually inspire other people to experience their own greatness. It is not so much a "doing" as an "allowing", "inspiring", "guiding" and "celebrating". You do this by providing an environment of safety and trust for people to be who they are. You provide them with the understanding and tools to be their greatest self. You invest in them as a person. And, most importantly, you allow them to fail without judgment or condemnation so they can grow.

12

WIN EVERY TIME
WITHOUT EXCEPTION

The only way to have a friend is to be one.
— Ralph Waldo Emerson

Up to this point, we have laid a number of important concepts that are necessarily to understand the overall point of "win every time without exception" and "be your most influential self". Let's review some of those points:

○ You are not your name or your body. You are consciousness — applying thinking and getting a corresponding result.

○ You don't experience life. You experience your thinking about life.

○ Thought is primary.

○ The quality of thought triggers the quality of emotion you experience.

○ Every emotion creates a dynamic physiological experience, starting with the shape of your heart rhythm.

- Your emotions determine which part of your brain you access.

- Every emotion has a frequency and signature.

- Your emotions make an energetic imprint in the environment.

- Your consistent and habitual thoughts and emotions create your current "emotional set point".

- You have an electromagnetic field that attracts experiences that match your state of "being".

- If you want to have different experiences, you must change your "state of being" by changing your thinking.

What does "win every time" mean? To me, it means having the best possible experience every time. In order to "win", or be in your highest possible state of thought, emotion, physiology, and being, you must want the highest and best outcome for the other person too.

If you don't want the best for the other person, you are not in a high quality thought and emotion. In fact, this is even more critical when we understand that your emotions affect other people, as described in the scientific studies conducted by HMI. You cannot want to "win" from a selfish state of "I win" and "you lose" in order to be in your highest thought/emotion/being state. You must have a win-win mindset for all concerned in order to achieve your own optimal state.

How to be your most influential self

○ Look for a win-win solution, experience or outcome in all situations.

○ If you haven't found a win-win solution, you haven't found a solution at all.

○ Invest in other people; what you put out energetically and emotionally, you will get back many fold.

○ Align yourself with what the other person wants; find the common ground.

○ See other people in the best possible light. This will literally "bring out the best" in them. You are an energetic being and your emotions program the environment so seeing the best in them, literally brings the environment to a higher frequency allowing them to access higher-level thoughts and emotions too.

○ Dwell on what you like about them (to the exclusion of everything else). When you focus on the highest attribute, it has a tendency to bring all other attributes up. (The reverse is true too. Never focus on someone's negative attributes. You are actually energetically reinforcing them and dragging their other qualities down too).

○ Forgiveness is for YOU, not the other person. If you experience your thoughts and corresponding emotions, when you hold something against someone else, you are the one getting that quality of experience. Forgive and forget as quickly as possible! (If you can not forget — at least "tell a new story" about the facts that occurred so you can use it to your benefit and theirs!).

13

POWER, PERFORMANCE, PRESENCE, & PERSUASION = P4

I dwell in possibilities.

— Emily Dickinson

○ You have power. You are power in action. It is built in to the system. You are an expression of the system. You cannot operate outside the system, although you can seem to have the experience of being disconnected from it.

○ Life performs according to your input via your thoughts and emotions.

○ Your presence or who you are being in any moment draws to you an exact matching experience based on the law of resonance. Truly, what you put out, you get back.

○ You are the power of persuasion. You persuade or program the environment according to your thoughts and emotions. You persuade other people according to your emotional set point or state of being. You have the ability to help others improve their emotional state when you are in a Loving, positive state yourself.

P4 is a formula that you can use to take your performance from potential to powerful performance. It is my honor to provide performance development training and emotional intelligence training to organizations to optimize their performance while reducing stress, turnover and mistakes and improving many other metrics. I also train individuals to apply and integrate these principles to completely transform their personal programming and life results.

PART 2

Tools, Tips, Techniques & Concepts

The best way out is always through.

— Robert Frost

This section is designed to give you tips, tools, techniques and concepts that you can utilize to transform your way of thinking and being. Many of these concepts were discussed in the book so this is designed to be a quick reference.

— Virtual Vision —

- Begin with the end in mind.

- Identify "who" you want to be.

- You can look to notable people in history or in your friends and family for inspiration.

- Identify the characteristics and traits of the person you want to be.

- Write a Virtual Vision explaining the scenario that would indicate that you have already had the experience of being that person. In other words, write it as though it has already happened.

- Remember to engage all of your senses in writing your Virtual Vision. You can use a romance novel as a great guide to get your juices flowing.

- "Put on" the characteristics of the person you want to be by recalling times when you experienced those characteristics in your life.

- "Feel as if" you are actually having the experience you have written right now.

- "Be" the person in your Virtual Vision in your thought, emotions and behavior.

- Put yourself in the scene of your Virtual Vision experiencing every sense as it is written.

o This is similar to the "I Am" concept. You are what you decide to be and persist in being.

o Burn the bridges — decide to truly commit to being this person. Be consistent and vigilant until you are this new person. Repetition is key.

o If you need motivation, remember your "why". No matter what you think your "why" is, it is always to experience Love.

o Read, rehearse and experience your Virtual Vision morning and night. It is particularly helpful to do this when you are in a drowsy or non-resistant state and your subconscious is more receptive.

A little background of how this works.

~ How you think and feel broadcasts an electromagnetic signature that influences every atom of your body.

~ Thoughts are electric. Thoughts send out the request.

~ Feelings are magnetic. Feelings draw back the experience that matches your "state of being".

~ Dr. Joe Dispenza says, "marry a clear intention (thought) with an elevated emotion."

~ The Bible says, "be clear and concerned." It also says, "as a man thinketh in his heart, so is he."

Neurological Rewiring

○ The average person has over 60,000 thoughts per day.

○ Most of these thoughts are the same or similar in quality or vibration to prior thoughts.

○ Thoughts that fire together, wire together and create neuropathways.

○ In order to create new thought patterns, you need to unwire or override the old thought patterns and install new thought patterns.

○ There is a certain amount of "glue" (nuero-growth factor) that holds your neurological wiring in place. As you install new neuro-pathways, the "glue" has to be taken from the old thought patterns and used to hold the new thought pattern in place. With repetition, you move all the "glue" from the old pattern and install it into the new pattern. At some point, the old thought pattern is no longer held in place. It has literally been dissolved and the new thought pattern is established.

○ When this has occurred, the new thought pattern is your new normal.

○ When you notice that you are triggered, "stop" thoughts and replace them with more positive thoughts. You can even use a random thought, like "I'm alive," as it serves to derail the negative thought process.

o In reality, the process is not about doing. It is "undoing". In your natural state, you are Loving, positive, and coherent. You are only removing disintegrative energies you have used to block your natural state.

Think of Yourself As An Energy System

o You are very much like an energy system or a battery.

o This is not a new age concept. A little practical thinking will proves it.

o You eat to gain energy.

o You sleep to restore your energy.

o When you have a small child asking you "why" constantly, you tell them to go run around and "burn off some energy."

o There are really only two types of energy that affect your system.

~ Love, coherence, restorative

~ Fear, entropy, incoherence, disintegrative

o Your emotions are a primary factor that affects your energy system.

o Positive thoughts build up your energy.

o Negative thoughts waste energy.

o   How you manage your energy system has tremendous implications on every aspect of your life, including your health.

Create A New Emotional Set Point

o   Everyone has an emotional set point.

o   This is "how you wake up in the morning".

o   This is your general or current state of being.

o   Your emotional set point is the culmination of your thoughts, emotions, behaviors, reactions, outlook, perception and mindset.

o   You can change your emotional set point by changing your thinking, which will have a corresponding affect on your emotions, perceptions, behavior and everything else.

o   Your emotions are a perfect feedback system to tell you what types of thoughts you have been thinking.

~   If you are feeling frustrated, you have been thinking low quality, low vibration, disintegrative thoughts.

~   If you are feeling joyful, you have been thinking high quality, high vibration, positive and Loving thoughts.

- Use the various techniques to improve your quality of thinking, which will improve your emotional set point until it is now your new normal.

- Self awareness
  - ~ Listen to your inner and outer conversation.
  - ~ Focus on how you feel
  - ~ Be aware of your state of being.

- Use thoughts that you believe to walk yourself up the emotional scale. Start from where you are and reach for a better feeling thought that you still believe.

- If you cannot grab a better feeling thought that you believe, you can say, "wouldn't it be nice if so-and-so were true." This at least takes you from doubt to possibility.

—— Tell A New Story ——

- Life has happened up to this point.

- Circumstances and facts have occurred.

- You use those facts and circumstances to tell a story.

- Is it a story you like?

- If it isn't a story you like, decide to tell a new story.

- You can use the same facts to tell a different story about learning, accomplishment, self-empowerment, and overcoming.

- You experience yourself. You are the experience. You experience the quality of story that you tell yourself as it is always playing in the background.

- Your life is a product of your story.

- Your life will continue to bring to you experiences that are of the same quality as the story you tell. This alone is motivation to tell a new story.

- In any situation, you can decide to be right or decide to be happy. You will get the corresponding result.

- Be for what you are for rather than against what you are against. Huh? Follow Mother Teresa's example. She would not attend an anti-war rally but was more than willing to attend a pro-peace event. Be an advocate for what you want and don't focus on its opposite.

—— Perception ——

- All experiences are neutral (fishing).

- You experience everything according to your thoughts, beliefs, emotions and perceptions.

o What someone else thinks of you is truly about him or her. They experience you according to their thoughts and beliefs. You can see this is true by virtue of the fact that everyone does not feel the same way about the same person.

o On the other hand, what you think about someone else is not about them. It is about you! When you judge someone to be a certain way, it is a sure sign that you need to look in the mirror and investigate why you think this way.

—— Love is the Royal Law ——

o As we learned in Dr. David Hawkins's book, *Power vs. Force*, every emotion has a vibration, a signature.

o Love is a very high vibration emotion.

o Love is highly coherent and unifying.

o Love is highly integrative and restorative.

o The Bible says, "A merry heart is like a medicine." This is due to the literal health benefits you experience when you hold this emotion beginning with a coherent heart rhythm, balanced ANS, accessing your higher brain functions and releasing DHEA (the vitality hormone) into your system.

o Love is your natural state before you put any

disintegrative energy into our system and create limiting thought patterns.

o Unconditional Love is a redundant statement. By its very nature, Love does not impose any conditions. Love just Is.

Meditation/Mindfulness/Heartfulness/Now

o While there are many different processes, the general idea is to quiet the mind and experience the present moment.

o Focus on your breathing

o Focus on your heart

o Drop your thinking and listen

o Drop resistance and thought and just feel

o Go into the silence

o Allow

o Be Here Now

o Feel connected to everything

Gratitude & Appreciation

o At any moment, you are only experiencing one emotional state.

o When you are intentionally grateful, you cannot be in a negative emotional state.

o Appreciation means to increase or grow. As you are grateful or appreciative, your vibration increases.

o Intentionally writing down what you appreciate will move you to a higher emotional set point.

o By writing down lists of what you are grateful for, you gain momentum.

Acknowledge Your Accomplishments

o By writing down your successes or accomplishments, you create momentum.

o Like attracts like. Accomplishments attract accomplishments.

o When you feel successful, you are in a vibration of success. More will come.

Thought Is Primary

○ You are always thinking. The quality of your thinking determines the quality of your life experience.

○ You may not have considered this, but you are always thinking even though you may use different terminology for this thinking. I've developed this list to show you different forms of thinking:

Gratitude ~ a thought about something you appreciate

Inspiration ~ thoughts that move you to action or change

Belief ~ repetitious thoughts that create a viewpoint

Fear ~ thoughts of harm or destruction; disintegrative

Judgement ~ comparison or blaming thoughts

Guilt ~ self-imposed blame or condemnation thoughts

Worry ~ repetitious thoughts expecting problems or disaster

Prayer ~ intentional, focused thought; sometimes a thought request

Forgiveness ~ a change in thought or releasing a thought

Mediation ~ slowing or stopping thought

o Every thought exists at a certain frequency and has a particular signature.

o The quality of your thinking is literally pre-programming your physiology and if persisted upon, the future experience that you will create.

—— Strike A Pose ——

o Our body language mirrors our emotional state.

o Assume a "power position".

o You can use a "hack" by assuming the body language of the emotion that you would like to experience and soon enough you will actually begin experiencing that emotion. This is based on groundbreaking Harvard research by Amy Cuddy.

—— Labels/Placebo ——

o Everything that you experience in life has a label: chair, book, apple, car, anger, etc.

o Often, once you have had an experience and define it in a particular way, you tend to experience your label rather than the actual experience.

o When you have a belief that something will have a particular affect, you experience that affect irrespective of its efficacy. This is known as the placebo affect. It is a self-fulfilling prophecy.

○ This is why we love first time experiences. We actually have the experience rather than repeating a thought pattern about it.

The Wisdom of the Heart

○ According to HMI, our heart and brain are in constant communication.

○ Over 80% of the impulses emanate from the heart.

○ Our intuition resides in our heart.

○ Our cultural sayings reflect the wisdom of the heart:

I knew it by heart.
It was heartfelt.
Let's get to the heart of the matter.
He won my heart.
His heart was in the right place.
He is a man after my heart.
Absence makes the heart grow fonder.
She is all heart.
Be still my heart.
Bless your heart.
Cross my heart.
Faint of heart.

○ According to Dr. Bruce Lipton, the heart measures energy and provides impulses as feedback whether we should take an action or not. If the action is going to add to our energy, the heart will give us an impulse to do it or go toward it. If the heart evaluates that something will actually deplete our energy, we will feel disconnected which is a signal that the heart is not attracted to that idea or situation.

Drop Resistance

○ What you resist, persists.

○ Actually, what you resist increases because you are giving it a lot of focus and energy even though it is in a negative direction.

○ While counter-intuitive, to allow and accept where you are is the starting point of change and improvement.

○ Grace is the state of Loving allowance, acceptance and knowing that all is well.

○ Don't push against what you don't want. Allow it. It will dissipate.

○ This too shall pass.

○ Resistance is interference to your natural state of being.

Communicating Through
Your Electromagnetic Field (HMI)

o Wherever there is electricity, a magnetic field is created.

o Your heart is electric so you have a magnetic field around you.

o You communicate through this electromagnetic field.

o Your emotions affect people in your environment.

o Your emotions can affect other people non-locally when you have a strong emotional bond with them.

o When you are coherent, or in an emotionally balanced state, your emotions can elevate other people in your environment.

o The most influential person in any situation is the one that is coherent and able to rule the energy exchange.

Win-Win

o You get what you think, whether wanted or unwanted.

o Any situation that you think is a win for you and a loss for someone else, is actually a loss for you because you are thinking low quality, competitive thoughts. This low quality thoughts will affect you, starting with your heart rhythm.

- Find solutions that are a win-win for everyone concerned.

- If it isn't a win-win, you haven't found the solution yet. Keep looking.

—— My Amazon's Alexa Analogy ——

- Amazon's Alexa makes for a great model to explain the conscious, subconscious and super conscious mind in operation.

Conscious

~ On a conscious level, you ask Alexa for information or give her commands.

~ You'll notice that the quality of your question or command determines the quality of her answer.

~ If you ask a poorly structured question, she says that the information is not available.

~ If you ask a clear, focused question, you get a useful answer.

Subconscious

~ Alexa's programs are similar to the subconscious mind.

~ Alexa has programs of information that you can access.

~ This is why she is able to tell you the weather forecast, history facts, addresses, music, etc.

~ This is similar to your thought patterns and beliefs that exist at a subconscious level. When stimulus happens, it triggers one of your subconscious belief patterns and creates a response/reaction.

~ For example, you might not be thinking about it, but if someone asks your dog's name, you pull it out of your subconscious and now it is at a conscious level when you tell the other person the name.

Super conscious
~ This is the system itself.

~ This is the 1s and 0s or the base program itself that makes it work.

--- Just for Fun ---

○ Let's look at the word "e-v-i-l". If you spell it backward, it is "l-i-v-e". When you live "backwards", you disconnect and are incoherent.

○ Let's look at the word "d-e-v-i-l". If you spell it backwards, it is "l-i-v-e-d". When you have been living "backwards", you reap the results in your experience.

○ Let's look at the word "disease". It is dis-ease or lack of ease. Lack of ease is stress. The medical community agrees that stress causes well over 90% of all diseases.

When you live without ease, you are more likely to get a disease.

○ Let's look at the word "righteous". Could it be the right-use of principles?

www.ingramcontent.com/pod-product-compliance
Lightning Source LLC
Chambersburg PA
CBHW071214220526
45468CB00002B/605